DISCARDED

Disgusting Body Facts

Itches and Scratches

Angela Royston

Raintree

Chicago, Illinois

www.heinemannraintree.com
Visit our website to find out more information about Heinemann-Raintree books.

To order:
☎ Phone 888-454-2279
💻 Visit www.heinemannraintree.com to browse our catalog and order online.

Edited by Nancy Dickmann, Sian Smith, and
    Rebecca Rissman
Designed by Joanna Hinton Malivoire
Original illustrations ©Capstone Global Library 2010
Original illustrations by Christian Slade
Picture research by Tracy Cummins and Tracey Engel
Originated by Capstone Global Library Ltd
Printed and bound in China by Leo Paper Products Ltd

14 13 12 11 10
10 9 8 7 6 5 4 3 2 1

Library of Congress Cataloging-in-Publication Data
Royston, Angela.
   Itches and scratches / Angela Royston.
      p. cm. -- (Disgusting body facts)
   Includes bibliographical references and index.
   ISBN 978-1-4109-3745-2 (hc)
   ISBN 978-1-4109-3751-3 (pb)
   1. Skin--Juvenile literature. 2. Itching--Juvenile
literature. I. Title.
   QP88.5.R6885 2010
   612.7'9--dc22
                                    2009022242

Acknowledgments
The author and publisher are grateful to the following for permission to reproduce copyright material: Alamy pp. **11**, **17**, **20** (©Medical-on-Line), **15** (©imagebroker/Kurt Möbus), **23** (©Bart's Medical Library/Phototake Inc.), **26** (©Nic Cleave Photography); Getty pp. **9** (©National Geographic/Darlyne A. Murawski), **21** (©Bill Beatty), **29** (©Darlyne A. Murawski); iStockphoto.com p. **28** (©Ales Veluscek); Photo Researchers, Inc. pp. **19**, **27** (©Dr. P. Marazzi), **25** (©SPL); Shutterstock pp. **7 bottom** (©Oberon), **12** (©Alan C. Heison), **13** (©Jessica Bethke); Visuals Unlimited, Inc. p. **7 top** (©Dr. Dennis Kunkel).

Cover photograph of a healing wound reproduced with permission of Photo Researchers, Inc. (©Edward Kinsman).

Every effort has been made to contact copyright holders of material reproduced in this book. Any omissions will be rectified in subsequent printings if notice is given to the publisher.

Some words are shown in bold, **like this.** You can find out what they mean by looking in the glossary.

Contents

Itchy Skin

Skin covers almost all of your body. Skin keeps out dirt and **germs** that can make you sick. It protects you from the sun. However, skin can sometimes itch. It can itch so much that it drives you crazy!

Did You Know?

Scratching can stop skin from itching, but scratching can also make things worse. This book will tell you why.

Itchy Head

Your head itches when your **scalp** is itchy. Your scalp is the skin below your hair. Your head may itch when you have:

- insects in your hair called head lice
- **dandruff**
- dirty hair and scalp
- shampoo left in your hair

dandruff

dandruff

scale

A hair is covered with
tiny **scales**. You can
only see them through
a microscope.

microscope

Head Lice

Head lice are insects that live in your hair. They bite your **scalp** and suck up some of your blood. The lice's **saliva**, or spit, makes your head itch. Their poo makes your head itch, too!

head lice

hair

Did You Know?
Head lice lay lots of eggs. The eggs hatch into more lice. Soon your whole head could be crawling with lice!

Dandruff

Your skin loses flakes of dead skin all the time. The flakes are too small to see. You get **dandruff** when the flakes clump together. They form big white flakes. Dandruff makes your **scalp** itch.

dandruff

The more this person scratches, the more dandruff she makes!

11

Sunburn

Too much sun harms your skin.
Sunburn makes your skin dry and itchy.
Large pieces of dead skin peel off.

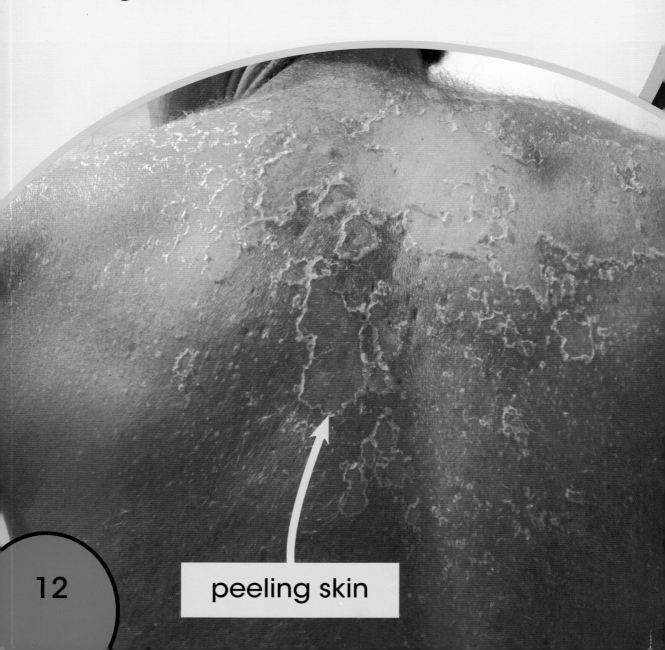

peeling skin

sunburn

WARNING

Sunburn is bad for your health. It can cause a dangerous disease called **skin cancer** when you are older. When you are out in the sun, remember to cover your skin and protect it with sunscreen.

13

Heat Rash

If part of your body is often hot and sweaty, you may get a heat **rash**. Lots of small red bumps will appear on your skin. Heat rash is very itchy!

heat rash

sweat

Did You Know?

Sweat oozes from your skin through tiny holes. The holes are called **pores**. You might get a heat rash when the pores become blocked.

15

Skin Allergy

Some people have a skin **allergy**. The allergy gives them itchy red marks called a **rash**. The rash may include little **blisters**. Scratching makes the rash worse.

rash

Did You Know?
Some of the things that people may be allergic to are:
- laundry detergent
- perfumed soap
- poison ivy
- cats
- wool

Food Allergy

Some people are **allergic** to certain foods. For example, eating peanuts may give them an itchy **rash**. The rash is often red and blotchy.

swollen lip

A food allergy can also make some people sick. Their lips might swell up. Their eyes might become red and itchy.

19

Chicken Pox

Chicken pox is an illness. You can catch it from someone who already has it. Chicken pox gives you an itchy **rash** on your body. Little red bumps change into **blisters**.

chicken pox

burst blister

When a blister bursts, the liquid inside oozes out. The liquid dries and forms a crusty yellow scab.

Warts

You can catch warts from other people. Warts are caused by **germs**. The germs get into your skin through tiny cracks. A wart forms a bump on your skin. It can last for months.

wart

plantar warts

A **plantar wart** is a flat wart on the sole of your foot. It can make your foot sore to walk on.

Athlete's Foot

Athlete's foot makes the skin between your toes itchy and **scaly**. Athlete's foot is caused by a **fungus**. A fungus is a small living thing, sort of like a plant.

Did You Know?

You can catch athlete's foot from someone who has it. You are most likely to catch it if your feet are often hot and sweaty.

This is a magnified photo of someone's toenail. You can see the athlete's foot fungus in red.

Scratching

Scratching can make a skin problem much worse. When you scratch, your nails scrape across your skin. Your nails make tiny cuts in your skin.

pus

Germs may get into the cuts. Then the cuts become red and sore. They may begin to ooze yellow **pus**.

More About Skin and Hair

The thinnest skin is on your eyelids.

Fine hairs grow all over your body. But they do not grow on the palms of your hands or the soles of your feet.

You have about 120,000 hairs growing on your **scalp**.

Shampoos can help! You can use special shampoos to get rid of **dandruff**. You can use special shampoos and combs to get rid of head lice.

comb

head louse

Glossary

allergy when you are very sensitive to something and your body reacts badly to it

blister swelling on the skin that is filled with liquid

dandruff white flakes of dead skin that form on your scalp

fungus small living thing. Mold and mushrooms are types of fungus.

germ tiny living thing that can make you sick if it gets inside your body

plantar wart type of wart. Plantar warts usually grow on people's feet.

pore tiny opening in the skin. Sweat escapes through pores.

pus thick yellow or white liquid that forms when a cut is infected by germs

rash red marks on the skin. Rashes can sometimes be itchy.

saliva liquid in the mouth. Saliva is also called "spit."

scale small, flat, hard piece of skin that protects the body

scalp skin on the top and back of your head. Hair grows from your scalp.

scaly covered in scales

skin cancer type of dangerous disease

Find Out More

Find out

Can pets get head lice?

Books

Glaser, Jason. *First Facts: Chicken Pox*. Mankato, MN: Capstone, 2006.

Royston, Angela. *How's Your Health? Allergies*. Mankato, MN: Smart Apple Media, 2009.

Taylor, Barbara. *The Best Book of the Human Body*. New York: Kingfisher, 2008.

Websites

http://kidshealth.org/kid/health_problems/index.html
Go to "Skin" to find out more about athlete's foot, eczema, rashes, and other skin problems.

www.aaaai.org/patients/just4kids
This web page for children tells you all about allergies. It includes games, puzzles, and videos.

www.headlice.org/kids/index.htm
This Website is full of facts, games, animations, and poems about head lice.

31

Index

32